WHAT EATS WHAT IN A DESERT FOOD CHAIN

ILLUSTRATED BY **ANNE WERTHEIM**

WRITTEN BY **SUZANNE SLADE**

PICTURE WINDOW BOOKS

a capstone imprint

From a prickly cactus to a quick coyote, all living things are part of a food chain. Each plant or animal in a food chain is connected, because each one eats the one before it.

The bright, sunny desert is full of plants and animals. Most food chains rely on sunlight. And in the desert there is plenty of it.

producer

An ocotillo plant stretches its long arms toward the sun. Bright red flowers bloom. A warm wind scatters the seeds.

Producers use sunlight, water, nutrients, and air to make their own food.

Soon the ocotillo loses all of its seeds and flowers. A kangaroo rat nibbles the crunchy seeds on the ground.

consumer, herbivore

A consumer eats plants or animals for energy. An herbivore eats only plants.

The kangaroo rat stops to rest.
A young rattlesnake waits and watches.

The snake attacks!

consumer,
carnivore

A carnivore eats only other animals.

The snake curls up in the sunlight. It isn't safe for long.
A hungry roadrunner zips by and snatches its next meal.

consumer, omnivore

An omnivore eats both plants and animals.

Darkness settles upon the desert, but all is not still ...

The coyote's glowing eyes spot prey.

Pounce!

consumer,
carnivore

The coyote is a strong hunter. But even *it* can become another animal's meal. One wrong step can bring a deadly snake bite.

A crested caracara quickly
finds the dead coyote.

consumer,
scavenger

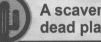 A scavenger eats mainly
dead plants or animals.

17

Not much is left of the coyote. The decomposers do their part. Beetles, bacteria, and fungi break down the rest.

decomposers

Decomposers break down dead plants and animals. Their waste is used as nutrients by plants.

Now the soil is rich for a new plant to grow.
The desert food chain will continue on.

FOOD WEB

Now that you've learned about one food chain, take a look at this food web of the Sonoran desert. A food web is made up of many food chains within a single place.

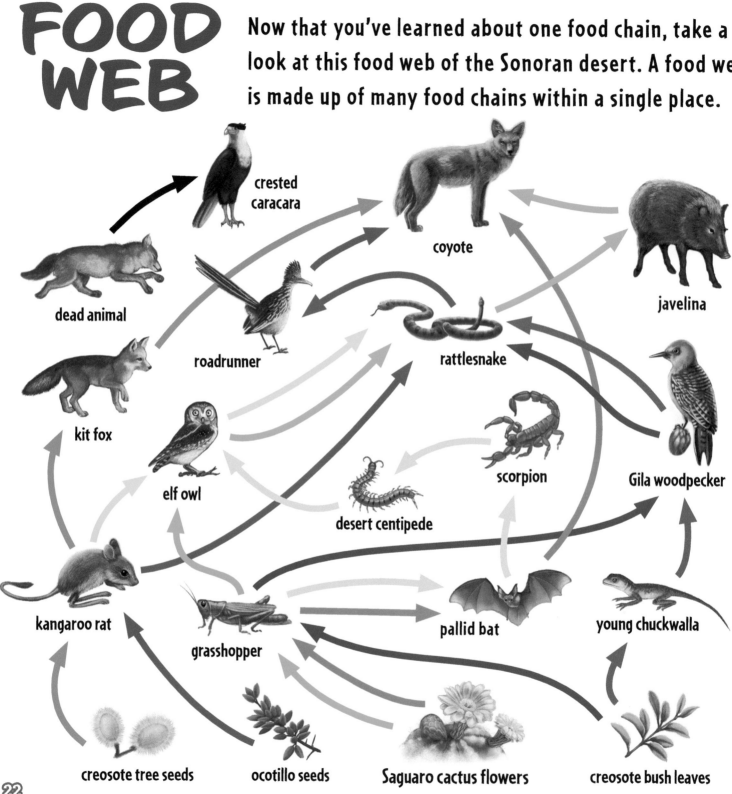

crested caracara

coyote

javelina

dead animal

roadrunner

rattlesnake

kit fox

Gila woodpecker

elf owl

scorpion

desert centipede

kangaroo rat

grasshopper

pallid bat

young chuckwalla

creosote tree seeds

ocotillo seeds

Saguaro cactus flowers

creosote bush leaves

GLOSSARY

carnivore—an animal that eats only other animals

consumer—an animal that eats plants or animals for energy

decomposer—a living thing, such as fungi or bacteria, that breaks down dead plants and animals

desert—a dry area with little rain in which the plants and animals have learned to live with small amounts of water

herbivore—an animal that eats only plants

nutrient—a part of food, such as a vitamin, that is used for growth

omnivore—an animal that eats both plants and animals

prey—an animal hunted by another animal for food

producer—a plant that uses sunlight, water, nutrients, and air to grow

scavenger—an animal that feeds mainly on dead plants or animals

READ MORE

Dahl, Michael. *Hot, Hotter, Hottest: Animals that Adapt to Great Heat.* Animal Extremes. Minneapolis: Picture Window Books, 2006.

Kalman, Bobbie. *How Do Living Things Find Food?* Introducing Living Things. New York: Crabtree, 2011.

Kalman, Bobbie. *What Is a Food Chain?* My World. New York: Crabtree, 2011.

INTERNET SITES

FactHound offers a safe, fun way to find Internet sites related to this book. All of the sites on FactHound have been researched by our staff.

Here's all you do:

Visit *www.facthound.com*

Type in this code: 9781404873865

Super-cool stuff! Check out projects, games and lots more at **www.capstonekids.com**

INDEX

LOOK FOR ALL THE BOOKS IN THE FOOD CHAINS SERIES:

WHAT EATS WHAT IN A **DESERT** FOOD CHAIN

WHAT EATS WHAT IN A **FOREST** FOOD CHAIN

WHAT EATS WHAT IN A **RAIN FOREST** FOOD CHAIN

WHAT EATS WHAT IN AN **OCEAN** FOOD CHAIN

Thanks to our advisers for their expertise, research, and advice:
Karen Krebbs
Conservation Biologist
Arizona-Sonora Desert Museum, Tucson

Terry Flaherty, PhD, English Professor
Minnesota State University, Mankato

Editor: Shelly Lyons
Designer: Alison Thiele
Art Director: Nathan Gassman
Production Specialist: Danielle Ceminsky
The illustrations in this book were created digitally.

Picture Window Books
1710 Roe Crest Drive
North Mankato, MN 56003
www.capstonepub.com

Library of Congress Cataloging-in-Publication Data
Slade, Suzanne.
What eats what in a desert food chain? / by Suzanne Slade ; illustrations by Anne Wertheim.
    p. cm. — (Capstone picture window books: food chains)
 Includes index.
ISBN 978-1-4048-7386-5 (library binding)
ISBN 978-1-4048-7690-3 (paperback)
ISBN 978-1-4048-7981-2 (ebook PDF)
1. Desert ecology—Juvenile literature. 2. Desert animals—Juvenile literature. 3. Food chains (Ecology)—Juvenile literature. I. Wertheim, Anne, ill. II. Title.

QH541.5.D4S53 2013
577.54—dc23

                        2012001133

Printed in the United States   5384